MW01702987

Bye Bye Baba
A Weaning Tale

A drawing book with original art by YOU!

By Nina Planck

Original art by:

What's it like when you're too big to nurse and your new baby brother comes home?

Find out how Matilda feels about saying "bye bye" to baba and hello to Luke.

Cover illustrations by Stanisław Wyspiański (Creative Commons)

ISBN: 978-0692894743
ISBN-10: 0692894748

Small Farm Press
NinaPlanck.com

smallfarm

For babies everywhere

Hi. My name is Matilda. I used to live in there, in mama's belly.

One day, it was time to come out. It was October 24th. That's my birthday!

I was *so tiny*. And I was so hungry!

When I wasn't hungry, I was awfully sleepy. (So was Mama.)

Daddy said I didn't do very much. I guess having milk from Mama was just about my favorite thing in the whole world. Sometimes, I just *had* to have some.

I called it "baba." Mama told me that other babies called it nummies, nunu, ninni, la-las, mounty-side, Mommy milk, muck, minutes, num-nums, nursies, nook, leche, mee-mees, dee-dees, na-nights, nuh-nuh, monk, dit-dow, ta-ta, beeboos, bob, um-yums, bobbies, bubbies, and The Boob.

And what do *you* call it?

Baby animals drink baba too. Animals who make milk are called "mammals." The fancy word for baba is "mammary." That sounds kind of like "mama," doesn't it?

One day, I was sitting on Daddy's lap, and I grabbed some of his food.

Food felt pretty funny in my mouth. And some of it tasted pretty good!

It wasn't anything like baba.

But pretty soon, I was playing with real food every day.

Sometimes, I forgot all about baba.

Sometimes, I was thinking about baba, but Mama wasn't. "That's only for naptime and bedtime," she said.

Meanwhile, I got really big and tall. Then a funny thing happened. Mama got bigger too.

Mama said it was time to say bye bye to baba. We had a party with lots of baba. Only it wasn't Mama's baba — it was a Bye Bye Baba cake!

After my party, I was *really* a big girl.

Then Luke showed up. That was on August 4th. Luke is my baby brother. Luke was *this* tiny.

Now Luke was getting all the baba.

Well, I guess that's what babies do. They don't do very much, do they?

But I'm a big girl, and I have lots of things to do.

The End

Martha and Peter's Tale or *Weaning a Toddler*

My son Peter and I both loved extended nursing. I feared weaning was going to be an ordeal, but it turned out to be surprisingly easy.

We weaned on his third birthday. To prepare, we talked about how he was finishing the mommy milk and how it was really meant for babies, since they couldn't eat food. By this point, we were nursing just three times a day: wake-up, nap, and bedtime—and only at home.

Perhaps being excited about his birthday helped. The night before, we had a special last nursing session and blew out a candle to say goodbye. I gave in at naptime the next day because he was crying. But that was it. He only asked for it one other time, which amazed me.

Instead of nursing at naptime, I'd lie down with him and we'd listen to a talking book. He only fell asleep sometimes, but was ready to stop napping anyway. We changed the morning routine by jumping right out of bed after a quick snuggle and making a treat of warm cow's milk with maple syrup (for about a week). Bedtimes were surprisingly ok.

I didn't worry about Peter getting enough dairy as he drank whole milk from a cup and ate plenty of full-fat yogurt.

All in all, it was an easy change. It was the right time for both of us. Good luck to all the weaning mothers!

Martha Wilkie
New York City, 2016

About the Author

"A cross between Alice Waters and Martha Stewart," (*Washington Post*), Nina Planck is the author of the acclaimed *Real Food: What to Eat and Why*. Her vigorous defense of traditional foods liberates eaters from low-fat and imitation foods.

In *Real Food for Mother and Baby*, Nina takes up traditional diets for mother, father, and child. She dismantles common misconceptions and fears about prenatal and weaning foods in her typically direct style.

Nina's cookbooks, the ebook *Farmers' Market Cookbook*, and the gorgeous hardcover *Real Food Cookbook*, offer delicious and simple recipes using real food. Nina lives in Greenwich Village and Stockton, New Jersey, with her husband, Rob Kaufelt, a cheesemonger, and their three children: Julian, Jacob, and Rose.

Her children's books are *The Numbers You Know: A Natural Counting Book* and *The Egg Book: A Child's Guide to Chickens, with Recipes*.

NinaPlanck.com

74893184R00029

Made in the USA
Middletown, DE
01 June 2018